POEMS with ATTITUDE UNCENSORED

To Eileen Armstrong and the pupils at Cramlington High School.
Thanks for fantastic feedback!

Acknowledgements:
Within Spitting Distance, Glue, The Professor of Philosophy, Ballad of Matt the Knife
and *Mr Rogers* first published in *Out of Order* (Evans, 2001).
The Egg Picker Upper first published in *The Moon Is On The Microphone*
(Sherbourne Publications 1997, 2000).
Betrayal first published in *The Rhyme Riot* (Macmillan 2002).
A version of *Scattering The Ashes* first published in *May The Angels Be With Us, Poems of
Life, Love, AIDS and Death* by Marc and Andrew Peters (Shropshire County Council, 1995).

First published in Great Britain in 2002 by Hodder Wayland,
an imprint of Hodder Children's Books.

2

Editor: Kay Barnham
Designer: Jane Hawkins

British Library Cataloguing in Publication Data
Peters, Andrew, 1965–
    Poems with attitude: uncensored
    1. Teenagers – Conduct of life – Poetry
    2. Young adult poetry, English
    I. Title II. Peters, Polly
    821.9'14'08'0353

ISBN 0 7502 4117 9

Printed and bound in Great Britain by Clays Ltd, St Ives plc

Hodder Children's Books
A division of Hodder Headline Limited
338 Euston Road, London NW1 3BH

POEMS With ATTITUDE
UNCENSORED

Andrew Fusek Peters
and
Polly Peters

HODDER
Wayland

Contents

LOVE

WITHIN SPITTING DISTANCE 7
TRENCH TACTICS 8
TURN-TABLE 10
THE PERFECT LAD 11
SKATE DATE 12
LOVE TRIANGLE 14
BRACE YOURSELF 15
I'M NOT (A)CROS(TIC) WITH YOU AT ALL 16
NO WAY 17
DUMPED 18
FRENCH VERBS 19

UP FRONT

SCRITCH 21
UNDER MY SKIN – SELF HARM 22
BETRAYAL 23
CRACKING NUTS 24
GOOD TO BE A LAD 25
DISTANT SHORES 26
ALL THE FUN OF THE *FESTER*VAL 27
SIZE MATTERS 28
SIZE MATTERS 2 30

SEX

ONAN THE BARBARIAN? 33
PERFORMANCE PRESSURE 34
QUIZ YOURSELF 36
THE NAMING GAME 38
THE FARAWAY TREE 39
CONDOM 40
THE RIVER 41

DRINK AND DRUGS

OUT OF PUFF 43
FIRST DRINK 44
IT'S LEGAL, SO THAT'S ALL RIGHT THEN 46
GLUE 47
VOMIT BLUES 48

RECIPE FOR DISASTER   50
UP TO SPEED   52
THAT'S THE SPIRIT   53
SORRY, AM I REPEATING MYSELF? (A PANTOUM)   54
MAD FOR IT   56

IT'S A SMALL WORLD

THE EGG PICKER-UPPER   59
MINIMUM WAGE   60
1948 – OR ANY DATE IN THIS ISLAND'S HISTORY   61
THE PROFESSOR OF PHILOSOPHY   62
PAPERS   64
POWERLESS OVER POLLUTION?   65
RED RIBBON – WORLD AIDS DAY   66
PHARMA-SUIT-ICAL   67

FAMILY

THE PERFECT PICTURE OF TACTFULNESS   69
FOR GRANDMA   70
PETAL   71
DARK SIDE   72
LARGIN' IT WIV ME PARENTS   73
OUR STEVE   74
KNIFE SONG   76
SCATTERING THE ASHES   78
A PERIOD COSTUME DRAMA   80
JUST   81

SCHOOL

DREAMING   83
BALLAD OF MATT THE KNIFE   84
IT'S ALL IN A NAME   86
MOOS AT TEN   86
CAT'S CRADLE   87
MR ROGERS   88
MR ROGERS 2   89
THE NIGHTHAWKS (AFTER EDWARD HOPPER)   90

NOTES FOR THE READER

FORMS   93
PERSONAL NOTES   94
ABOUT THE AUTHORS   96

LOVE

WITHIN SPITTING DISTANCE

Pucker those lips, prepare to dive,
Brush those teeth 'til they feel alive,
Take a breath, fill up your lungs,
Ready for the race of teenage tongues.
Round and round like a washing machine,
Until you encounter Nick O'Teen.
By gum, it's time to stop and think
And ban his brain-dead, bad-breath stink.
Admit it girl, it wouldn't go far,
Chuck him out and say tar-tar!
The race is lost, this boy's a mutt,
Who wants to snog a cigarette butt?

TRENCH TACTICS

IN THE NO-MAN'S LAND outside the loos,
Opposing camps are drawn up
Rude rumours have flown.
Boy then girl pushed forward.
First shots are fired:
"Fancy a movie?"
"Suppose."
They retreat to their ranks to interrogate
The code of flashing eyes and mumbled
  response.
Later that night:
The sentry guides them with torchlight
To velvet trenches.
The film begins with a barrage of sound
  and light,
And the boy's arm lumbers like a tank over
  the back of the chair
To land on the enemy's shoulder.
Yes! Yes! Yes!
He has entered the bottle zone.

Her head swivels. He moistens his tongue.
  She swallows spit.
They engage. ATTACK! ATTACK!
  IT'S A HEART ATTACK!
Teeth clash like armour plating.
Spit bombs fly between mouths.
Necks are targeted with biting precision.
His wounded tongue (he bit it earlier through
  nerves)
Responds to resuscitation.
Mates whoop while punters
Tut-tut like machine-gun fire.

What was the movie about? Who cares?
They troop out into the night,
Neck wounds dressed with scarves
To foil spying parents.
This was SNOGGING FOR VICTORY!

TURN-TABLE

"You must be tired, love!"
"Why?" I say,
"Cos you've bin runnin' thru' me mind all day!
And your dad's a burglar, stealing stars!
He must 'ave bin all the way to Mars!"
"Why's that?" I ask in mock surprise.
"To stick 'em in your sparklin' eyes!"
He leers, and leans against the doors,
I raise my eyes in silence, pause...
"Get your coat, you've pulled!" I smile,
Now watch him run a minute mile!

THE PERFECT LAD

The lad for me has teeth so white,
It's obvious he's Mr Right;
He'll know that I have got a brain,
"Let's talk!" will be his main refrain,
And not about the sporting score,
But **feelings, poetry,** and more.
His hands won't head towards my skirt,
He'll even cry when he is hurt.
He'll change his boxers every day,
His biceps! Oh, they'll make me sway!
He'll have such perfect, spotless skin,
His clothes will not be out, but in.
But such a lad is just a rumour,
I'll make do with a sense of humour.

SKATE DATE

This the day that anything can happen.
I have embarked on my skateboard
And am soaring over this blue summer
At a cruising altitude of ten centimetres.
My heart is in take-off.
Got a number in my pocket,
A phone in my bag and a date in my turbulent head.
This is the day that anything can happen.
All in a moment,
In the school corridor, with a blush
That bloomed on my face like an unsure flower,
My mates egging me on,
And me scrambled up with fear,
I stuttered one simple question
While praying for the answer.
And for once, on the day that anything could happen,
It did.

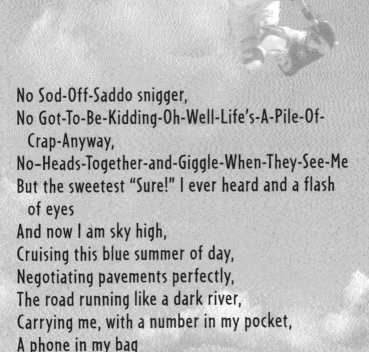

No Sod-Off-Saddo snigger,
No Got-To-Be-Kidding-Oh-Well-Life's-A-Pile-Of-
   Crap-Anyway,
No–Heads-Together-and-Giggle-When-They-See-Me
But the sweetest "Sure!" I ever heard and a flash
   of eyes
And now I am sky high,
Cruising this blue summer of day,
Negotiating pavements perfectly,
The road running like a dark river,
Carrying me, with a number in my pocket,
A phone in my bag
And my heart beating like a ring tone
On the day that anything can happen.

LOVE TRIANGLE

He says it's 'cos I feel rejected!
Pray his privates be bisected! May his spots
  be multiplied
And his swagger sub-divide.
It isn't hard to calculate
The adding up of all my hate:
Subtract regret and add derision
Forever between us, Long Division.
Who cares what planet he was on?
As for me? Well, Polygon.

BRACE YOURSELF

Now call us a pair of anoraks
Sporting identical train tracks
When we smooch, our steel-capped faces
Make sparks fly thanks to our braces
But now I'm going really mental
'Cos my boyfriend's orthodental.
As we furnurkled, just my luck,
That this snogging got us stuck!
An hour's canoodling I don't mind,
But not eternally entwined!
That kiss! The costly price we paid
Resulted in the fire brigade:
Gnashing like a pair of nutters,
Freed at last by wire cutters.

What next?

My boyfriend's had his tongue stud done.
Magnetic tongues. That will be fun!

I'M NOT
(A)CROS(TIC)
WITH YOU AT ALL

Dear Richard, don't worry about the mess,
It was only my most expensive dress.
Can I meanwhile compliment you on your
Khaki pants and combat vest? Phwooooar!
However, I have to say that despite
Envying your sense of style, I just might,
And I do hope this is OK,
Delay our next date for another day.

NO WAY

Can't stand him, I loathe him, detest and despise,
I hope he might meet an untimely demise.
Can't bear him, don't like him, I couldn't care less,
He's a nothing, a no one who doesn't impress.
Yet though he's as sexy as deep-frozen cod
He seems to believe he's a gift-packaged god.
I'm impervious now, he's a bucket of slime,
He can stick all his chat-ups where the sun doesn't shine.
A creep and a dull, insignificant bore,
A delusional git, self-obsessed to the core.
I'm a fool who just fell for his jet-propelled gob,
But this prince is a frog-featured, pond-dwelling slob.
He's a liar and scum-bag who said he would ring
But I bet he'll just boast of a one-night-stand fling.
He's a pus-bucket, a greaseball, a fatherless son (get it?),
Forget it, he's history, it's over and done.
I'd far rather spend lots more time on my own
Than waste any more thought... Oh, my God! It's the phone!
"Er... really... the party... enjoyed it... you what?
Tomorrow...? Well, maybe... Er, sure, yeah! Why not."

DUMPED

My heart is playing truant since you dumped me.
Lessons yawn and hours drag their feet
Until I see you in the corridor
And I am a ghost, see-through.
Look! Put your hand in my chest and it's empty.

My tears got in trouble again,
Excluded from my eyes
At just the moment when everyone saw
And the class exploded in a laughing bomb.

Now,
My smiles skive off my face
And ugliness follows me like a shadow.
Falling in love!
Hah!
That's for swots of softness,
Teacher's pathetic pettings.
And love is a swear word,
Dug into toilet doors
And hope is in detention
Writing over and over:

>   I won't do it again
>   I won't do it again
>   I won't do it again

FRENCH VERBS

Tomorrow, I will see him.
Erique. He will smile and
We shall sit together on the coach
To some historic castle.
We will be paired,
Like swans on a moat.

Today, we hold hands at the back,
Snatch moments in the shadows of stairs.
I bury my face against his scarf,
He whispers in French and I breathe him –
The smell of cigarettes, incense, vanilla,
Like autumn smoke.

Yesterday, he left.
Our breath froze as we said goodbye.
He gave me his scarf and half a pack of Gauloise
And we each kept a picture of us two
In the Boots photo booth.
As the coach pulled away,
The windows steamed up.
I could hardly see him wave
And the day was grey
As sackcloth.

UP FRONT

SCRITCH

This a^{djusti}ng, done by boys
Is gross exhibitionism
It really annoys!

Now Bertie Horrocks liked a fiddle,
Gave his trousered bits a twiddle.
Cricketers rub and rap stars scratch
Their pocket billiards – game, sweat and match!
Justified young Bertie Horrocks,
As he played with Betty Swollocks.
He scraped by night and itchy day
Until he scritched himself away.
Next day he took a little peek
"Oh, woe!" He gave a high-pitched squeak,
He searched, but there was nothing there,
'Twas vanished into thinnest air...

The moral of this tale of Bert
Is that he got his just dessert:
Now he is worried, somewhat sick,
Has anyone out there Spotted Dick?

UNDER MY SKIN – SELF HARM

You laugh at me when I am quiet
Until I snap and round with spite on you;
Inside my veins, these feelings riot,
Course my blood and colour me blue.

Roll up my sleeve, see your name
Scribbled on skin with a pen
That uses blood. This is no game
Of words that cut again and again.

I score myself and plough my arm
For the bitter harvest. In this way
I garner glances of alarm –
Better than being ignored each day.

Some call this gouged graffiti cruel,
But I have learned these words at school.

BETRAYAL

Like rollerblades, we make a pair
Watch us practise; with such flair

Pavements fly beneath our feet
In this kingdom of concrete
The original polyurethane pals
Surfing down suburban hills
Gossip, giggle, God, it's great
To hang around with my best mate.

But my best mate's become a spy,
Sold my secrets. I blink my eye
And he has gone to the other side.
The gang ride by; I try to hide,
Cover my feelings with concrete.
As pavements fly beneath my feet

I climb the hills of hurt and hate

To get away from my best mate.

CRACKING NUTS

They call me ill,

The breakdown boy, you know, one of them

As they put their finger to their head

Twirl it like a gun,

To indicate I'm wrong.

And I am,

For in the morning when I wake,

There is no reassuring this is day, get up, get on

But just a heavy fear,

An out-of-focus, lack of grasp

And I am gasping for meaning.

Death, to this sixteen year old

Is round the corner, over the road. I take pills to hide

   His face,

But medication only slows…

I slur and stumble like a fool,

The jester who doesn't get the joke.

GOOD TO BE A LAD

Give us a bench on the pavement
That is home for the evening,
Where hours dawdle like shuffling shoppers
And we dine out on meaningless banter
Served with crappy lavatorial puns.
Let us hold serious debates
On midfield tactics, trainers to go into debt for,
Gadgets with overwhelming numbers of
  strange knobs,
Cars whose turbo thrusts punch holes in the ozone,
And top-ten lists of girls in Year 10.
Give us action movies where bad guys get it bad
And die in multiples of ten
And good guys kick huge arse, then get the girl.
And at last,
Give us late-night take-aways in a freezing square,
Each chip an instant hot-water bottle,
Savouring the good life, the smooth time,
The sweet hours
Of being a lad.

DISTANT SHORES

Don't pretend you understand,
Nod, or try to take my hand.
Don't patronise me with that *look*,
Say, "I can read you like a book!"
You can't, not now, not then, not ever,
Believe me, you are not that clever.
"Teenage angst" is not my label,
I won't fit that tidy fable.
I'm in here and you're outside.
You're the cliffs and I'm the tide.
You don't know me any more,
To you I'm now a distant shore.
I stand alone on shifting sand
And you will NEVER understand.

ALL THE FUN
OF THE **FESTER**VAL

I live in the borough of **Acne**, Norf London

Wiv my **splatt**-mate

Who says every morning,

"Where'**zit** at?"

Yesterday,

When my **carbuncle** broke down,

I had to **pores** and think what to do.

Six **scabs** went by, but none stopped.

I was in a tight **spot**,

Bit of a **squeeze**

But finally caught the **pus** into town,

And went out for a lovely **pizza-face**.

SIZE MATTERS

I am treading water, just thirteen,
Drowning in a distinct lack of puberty,
Dreaming of armpit hair.
On this Californian beach
I am a swaying, skinny poplar
Surrounded by bronzed, bicep-bound oaks.
And every movie, magazine and myth I've seen
And read says
Boys like me don't get the girl,
But flounder about on the edge of the action.
And every movie, magazine and myth and
  boy's banter
In the shower room, behind the sheds, scribbled in
  stinking toilets
Says:
Size Matters.
And what they don't tell you in biology
Is that cold sea water
Shrinks even king-sized prawns to little shrimps.
But all these guys bouncing up and down this beach
Seem to have whole sperm whales packed away in
  their trunks.

And every crappy movie, dirty mag and lonely myth
Says:
I'm just small fry. And I believe the lie.
So today, instead of a gun,
I am packing a pair of socks.
As the waves crash,
I tumble and turn in this huge washing machine,
Hoping for no lost sock.

And for once,
When I stride from the surf
I'll sock it to 'em,
Win the battle of the bulge
And dream, dream, dream of growing up
To be like the movies and magazines and myths
  and men who say:
Size Matters.

SIZE MATTERS 2

I am a jellyfish stranded in the changing room,
Buffeted by the bustle of bristling bodies.
I shrink inside my faded orange bath towel
And hover in the slipstream of the shower queue.
Perhaps I won't be noticed
And the teacher will absent-mindedly assume I've
  just passed through.
But no, she's there, with register and pen,
Ticking one by one:
"Hang your towels on the hooks. Take your time.
The idea is to get clean,
Not see you if can dodge through without
  getting wet!"
She even keeps a list of "dates"
To counter all the "can't shower today, miss!"
  claims.
So, like sheep at the abattoir gate, each drops
  their towel and disappears,
Some blushing, some brazen.
My downcast eyes creep sideways:
"Oi! What you lookin' at? You a lezzie then?"
But every glance has only told me:
Size matters.

Shapes and curves easily defined as
'A cup', 'B cup' swell to
Defeat and deflate my double AAs.
"Fried Eggs!" laugh the boys in school,
"If you had no feet, you wouldn't wear shoes,"
They say, pinging the straps of my tiny bra.
And every joke, every up-and-down look repeats:
Size matters.

A few more shuffling steps.
My turn. Deep breath. Head down.
I close my ears to any shoals of giggles.
At least the fog of steam is welcoming.
I wrap myself in it
And dream that someone, someday shatters
The myth that:
Size matters.

ONAN THE BARBARIAN?

This isn't a sin,

And I find,

Such pleasure doesn't

Make me blind.

Wish I could

Believe the fact,

There's nothing sad

About this act.

Dress rehearsal

For someday,

By myself,

But that's OK.

PERFORMANCE PRESSURE

Raise a toast to the boast
You really should have done it
30 times down an alley
In the dirt lift the skirt
Against the wall, 30 seconds
That's all.
He lives for the boast in the boy's loo
Tell a tattle tale, is it true?
Do we care? Bin there,
And if you ain't, how very quaint and sad,
You'll never be a lad.
This is the pressure
Of the chat-up and the booze, cruise,
Dance-mix tricks,
The shout above the din,
Where you bin all my life?
Now you get it down yer neck
Til yer brain's a total wreck
It's a one-night fling –
Did he use anything?
Safe sex, what a joke,
He's the wham-bam bloke.

Be me, ah me, I ain't a he-man, man
Wanna wait for the date,
Listen to the word to get heard
In my heart make a start
With a flashing of the eye
In the night walk-talk.
Get to know each other in the flow
And there's plenty to do
Before we go all the way, no way,
Exploring with our hands
In different distant lands,
Betting on the petting
It's pleasure not pressure.
Raise a toast to the trust
That you don't need to do it 'til you're ready,
Take it steady
In the rhythm of love.

QUIZ YOURSELF

Considering the final move to prove your heart is his?
Grab a moment, have a break, take time to do a quiz.

YES NO
☐ ☐ **Do you think you'll be more popular if you go ahead?**

YES NO
☐ ☐ **Do you fear that you'll be left out, if you don't leap into bed?**

YES NO
☐ ☐ **Do you want to seem more grown-up and think he'll love you more?**

YES NO
☐ ☐ **Are you set on breaking age-rules relating to the law?**

Think you're ready? Really ready? Are you ready yet?
Feeling heady, going steady? On your marks, get set.

YES NO
☐ ☐ **Has he said that if you loved him, you would prove it, no delay?**

YES NO
☐ ☐ **Do you think he'll never leave you if you answer right away?**

YES	NO	
☐	☐	Do you feel the label 'virgin' is uncool and one to ditch,
☐	☐	In case you're labelled frigid, icy maiden or tight bitch?

Think you're ready? Really ready? Are you ready yet?
Feeling heady, going steady? On your marks, get set.

YES	NO	
☐	☐	Do your friends all boast about it, keeping scores on endless dates?
☐	☐	Is it likely that your boyfriend wants to brag to all his mates?
☐	☐	Does the thought of talking condoms cause a blushing, cringe-reaction?
☐	☐	Does the issue of respect concern you even just a fraction?

Time to count the scores now. Ready, steady, go?
If you've answered mainly YES, then consider saying NO!

THE NAMING GAME

Dick, tool, John Thomas, willy –
Inoffensive, even silly.
Nob, winkle, trouser snake –
Such names are not so hard to take.
Todger, wanger, words that lend
Humour to a man's best friend.
Vile expletives? Terribly lewd?
More of a giggle, not overly rude.

Now switch the gender, try to find
Which euphemisms spring to mind.
A dictionary won't help the hunt
For 'lady's bottom (at the front)'.

THE FARAWAY TREE

Back of car. Too far. Says who?
The mother whose car he's borrowed?
The father who told her to not be late?
But they love each other. Don't they?
And anyway it was really nice, sort of.
And it's not as though they hadn't talked
Or planned.
So why the breath of distance?
What they have done
Now hangs between them like laden branches.
Her grandad used to bring her walking here
And tell her of the Faraway Tree.

She traces a heart in condensation.
He stares at the steering column.
"So, you're OK? Did you...? Do you...?"
"Yeah, sure." She turns and smiles,
Sees his jaw and hands unclench.
One arm closes round her while the other,
Clumsily in capitals, draws across the window:

"There," he sighs. "I mean it."
And he does.

CONDOM

1.
That nervous night with you,
Unwrapped and willing to be worn;
Limp fears thrown aside
Clothing passion
With a glow.

2.
My brother scorns the rain,
Willing to bear the storm;
Consequence is hail
The size of sorrow,
And the scythe of the rainbow
Shall hunt him.

3.
There were nights
I threw the mad dice,
Risking all.
My luck held good,
But my brother, the gambler,
Has scattered his debt
In ashes.

THE RIVER

Takes him by the hand,
Upstairs to where she has hidden a river.
He almost stutters in her room, but she is gentle,
Helps him wade into the water. Hot.
She strips, dives under the duvet of dark.
And quickly, turning away,
Hiding his shame, he follows.
They kiss,
Her lips are waves running to the shore,
Their bodies are unsure,
Then touch with a ripple,
O the Oars stroking deep water now,
Where is the harbour?
Why doubt and fear this place?
As strong currents pull them
Down where feeling is all,
Rock the boat with smile and sigh
As he holds her and she holds him,
They are turning, tipping, river rushing in,
Over, yes overboard they sink but breathe underwater
And dying and living not drowning
No, no, this is air and another world

And perfect silence.

DRINK
and
DRUGS

OUT OF PUFF

When my lungs went on a protest march
To stop the torture;
When the fur coat on my tongue
Was sold at Sotheby's for ten grand;
When Laurence Llewellyn-Bowen
Tried to copyright the colour of my teeth;
When my breath got so bad
It was done for disturbing the peace;
When it took
One tent, two years' supply of Mars Bars
  and three teams of Sherpas...
To climb the stairs;
When I fell for cancer's crap chat-up line
and next thing I knew, he was all over me...
Then I finally sussed
I was a few fags short of a packet
And smoking (I'm not joking)
Was the *habit to die for.*

FIRST DRINK

There was a boy who was a boy
In the dark Slovakian night
Rasping on a rough tobacco
Dragging crows into his lungs
Coughing halos, burning now
For a drink to kill his thirst
It's his first, this two-pint glass
Filled with froth and foaming waves
He's a tide, he'll come on strong
Swallow down the spirit song
In a pub upon a hill
Wooden benches, starry roof,
Now he has his swaying proof
He tries to stand with all his will

But all of time is standing still, still
And he collapses, house of cards
As from his lips shoot shooting stars
Constellation of a spew
Blacking out, how he will rue
The day, oh rue the day
He drank his first drink, thirsty,
Cursing as he's carried home
To a cabin in the wood
Lay him softly on the bed
There was a boy, an English boy
Eleven years old with a mouth of gold
Tasting all his future fate
In the dark Slovakian night.

IT'S LEGAL, SO THAT'S ALL RIGHT THEN

In the year 1990, in civilized UK,
Let simple death statistics have their say:
Cannabis – zero, ecstasy – three,
But thirty-thousand boozers in eternity.

Who comes top with the highest score?
Not smack at sixty-two or Methadone,
  eighty-four.
Guess who wins the kick-the-bucket bet?
At one hundred and ten thousand, it's…
  Mr Cigarette!

The politician says he understands,
But industry has tied his hands,
"Let's demonize drugs! But drink?
  Come off it!
Forget the principle, look at the profit!

"We need this tax, such welcome wealth
Covers the costs of our poor health
And being British, we'd surely miss
The blackouts, fights, the vomit and piss."

GLUE

I have bought glue to stick together
What has fallen apart. Foul weather
Lends this concrete car park
A backdrop of dripping dumb down dark.
Time dawdles its frantic feet, drags
As we suck on plastic shopping bags
Breathe the fume that burns the brain.
Oblivious now to the singing rain,
We stagger down the echoing well
Under the weight of the sickening spell
Where clouds have stuck the sky together,
And broke our hearts in this foul weather.

VOMIT BLUES

Don't know about you
But when I've had a few
Have to head for the loo

With my palette of puke
It's a rainbow rebuke
From the diced-carrot duke

And no, I'm not thick
I'm the sultan of sick
And trickling's my trick

You think I'm a fool
Don't you know that it's cool
To dribble and drool?

So what If I sway?
It's so sexy to spray
And my mates go Wahay!

I'm the chairman of chuck
Yes, you'd better duck
From my fountain of muck

Now don't be a bore
As I fall through the door
Let's have just one more

I'm the alcopop king,
I slur as I sing
And athletically sling
With a:

Bleeeeeeeurrrrgh!

RECIPE for DISASTER

A pinch of fag smoke,
In fact, forget a pinch,
Think: empty the entire packet and slowly ferment.
Whack in lashings of loud music
'til everybody's shaken and neighbours are stirred.
(Carefully remove parents beforehand).
In the meantime, you will need dough and a willing
   older sibling.
 Mix in a dash of drinks that don't mix on empty stomachs
  (Especially the sweet strong stuff that makers insist
   isn't aimed at teens. My arse.)
   Add over-ripe cheesy chat-ups
    To spice up the proceedings.
     Wait until the mix is slurry and blurry,
      Then stir your partner's mouth with your tongue
       (This is best done with a slow whisking motion
          With regular opportunities to come up for air.

However, boys should exercise caution
In case their mixture goes stiff.
This is a much later stage – see under PSHE).
Pour in a fumble of fairly innocent hands
(Again, below the waist is not a recommended recipe
As it will lead to a serving of "Serves-You-Right-Slap-
   In-The-Face"),
Close windows and bake until one.
It is quite normal that the mixture now collapses,
Leaving a somewhat messy sleepover snog pudding
With snorers laid out like sponge fingers
Breath rising like yeast in the night.
The following morning expect headaches.
Add a soupçon of unexpectedly early-returning parents
To finish you off
When they go totally after dinner **mintal**.

This is **Cookery with Attitude**.

s

d

r

i

B

Like

Fly

Words

My

All

High

Now

Shy

Once

Shut

Science

Con-

Cut

Or

Mirr-

Need

My

Fill

Will

Speed

Of

Line

This

UP TO SPEED

THAT'S THE SPIRIT

This is:
Hand's best mate
Lip's kisser
Stomach's heater
This is:
Bottle's bottle
Nerve's distiller
Word's puller
This is:
Confidence kick-start
Tongue's turbo-charger
Flirt's fast car
This is:
Laughter's migration,
Chance's best chance
Late night's dreaming
This is:
Bladder's terrorist
Regret's lover
Head's Hammerer
This is
This is
This is

SORRY, AM I REPEATING MYSELF?

(A PANTOUM)

This dope is doing me in,
A somewhat squidgy black,
The jokes are a little bit thin
But we're having a giggle attack.

A somewhat squidgy black
It's going down a treat
We're having a giggle attack,
Now we need something to eat!

It's going down a treat
As we burgle the fridge for more
I still need something to eat,
Let us nip out to the store.

We burgle the fridge, what's more
The munchies have got us bad,
So let us nip to the store,
And see what fun's to be had.

The munchies have got us bad
And we stagger and sway in the street
Let's see what fun's to be had –
Oh, no, there's the Bill on the beat!

We try not to sway in the street,
But our paranoia's intense,
When stopped by the Bill on the beat,
Whatever we say must make sense!

Though our paranoia's intense,
He hasn't noticed, thank God
Whatever we said made sense!
And off he goes on the plod.

He hadn't noticed, thank God
The joke is now wearing thin
My brain is beginning to plod.
This dope is doing me in!

MAD FOR IT

I have gone mad, but we must stash this word,
The warmth of skunk, amphetamine thrill
And acid blur no longer work.
I have gone mad,
My mother leads me by the hand,
Prescribing doctors understand,
I swallow pills to numb what is already numb.
I have gone mad,
Such horrors flower in my head,
I must be confined to bed,
And on the ward,
I hear the schizophrenic screams.
My girlfriend comes, but as I shake,
She can no longer take
Such change in the laughing boy she knew.

Like shock, she pulls away,
And I am left with the long ache of day.
I have gone mad,
At school, the loony whispers grow,
Though some bring grapes,
Small bunches of love in their hearts.
Perhaps I shall grow well,
Today, I'm mad with me,
Believing every uttered lie
In the shallow cools of getting high.
How I shall miss the dealing out of
Sofa-sinking slur and sway.
But this was mad and made me mad
And on this psyche ward,
The breakdown lost-it elemental boy
Wonders if he has made a hash,
And searches, searches for the spirit's stash.

IT'S A
SMALL
WORLD

THE EGG PICKER-UPPER

Which came first,
The egg or the chicken?
Listen to this tale,
And let the plot thicken...

Once on the farm
The chicken scratched,
Found a barn
For eggs to hatch.

Eggs for chicks
And eggs on toast,
Chicken lived well,
A tasty roast.

The farmer smiled,
Though times were hard,
As bird ran free
Throughout the yard.

Times changed:

There was a man,
An egg-picker-upper,
He'd never again
Eat eggs for his supper.

Four thousand chickens,
All in one shed,
Some of them squawking,
Some of them dead.

Day was outlawed,
Lightbulb reigned,
Farmer vanished,
Birds well-trained.

Backs scratched raw,
Bleeding and sad,
This egg machine
Has gone quite mad.

And when their
Laying days have flown,
A pet-food tin
Is their final home.

The chicken, or the egg,
Which came first?
Who really cares,
For the bird that's cursed?

MINIMUM WAGE

Stood up
All day,
I earn the ache in my feet
And the cheap smile, stapled to my lips.
Today, some luck – a leftover lunch.
I sit outside the back door.
Four hours more,
Then bus to my bedsit
For food and sleep.
The boss drums on about teamwork –
I look at his suit and wonder.
We squabble over tip-division,
But a bit of a quid is sod-all.
The height of our shift
Is a stolen dessert.

When custom is quiet,
For a second, we breathe,
And I dream
Of more
Than the
Minimum.

1948 - OR ANY DATE IN THIS ISLAND'S HISTORY

I am not welcome,
That much is plain.
"No passport, no permit."
I try to explain:

"My family's in danger,
My country's gone wrong,
My father's best friend
Was publicly hung!

"With his daughter
We were made
To dig the grave
In which he laid."

The man's reply is:
"Are you a spy?"
His soul is suspicious,
His thin lips are dry.

All of us squeezed
Into one single room,
Layered like strudel
In the paraffin gloom.

I walk down the street.
A woman mutters:
"Do we need these
Foreign nutters?"

Romans, Vikings,
Celts and Jews,
All have sung these
Country blues.

Washed up on this
Island shipwreck
Register me as
Vera Fusek.

THE PROFESSOR OF PHILOSOPHY

We must stay! said the student,
And more was learned in a day,
Than all his lean years.
Posters were printed for the people.
But soldiers were kingfishers,
Darting through dissent.
They were swift, and his friends not quick enough.
He had the luck of the minnow.

That night,
He smuggled himself back to his father's house,
And did not leave for five forgetful years.
His mother, the cookery tutor,
Was happy to store him in the larder.
The father fabricated false partitions,
And the hours were slowly consumed.

By day, his father scoured libraries
And stole his boy an education.

By night, he crept into the living room,
Stuffed blankets into the piano
And forged his silent sonatas.

The country stopped.
Eyes and lips were careful.
Neighbours could be more than instruments
  of gossip.
Borders grew tight as drums,
Beating out the rhythm of the east.

Five years fled, like refugees.
His teeth rotted for lack of pantry-visiting dentists.
The train-dispatcher father
Built a coffin out of card,
Laid it in a bed of coal
And soused it in vinegar to put dogs' noses
  out of joint.

His son folded himself into that dark envelope,
Without a kiss.
The lid was sealed,
And as the steam train shuffled slowly West,
He wondered if success would always smell so sour.

PAPERS

The soldiers are working the café crowd
With pistols in belts and starched peak caps
It's easy to see: they are not nice chaps.
This fear in my stomach must not be allowed
To grow: "Why are you here? When did you arrive?"
Our papers demanded, flicked through, checked,
They saunter away, our day out is wrecked
In Prague in 1985.

"We must not let these terrorists win!
Identity cards are worth the cost
Though civil liberties are lost,"
Reply our leaders to the din.

Stopped in the street: "So who are you?"
United Kingdom, 2002.

POWERLESS OVER POLLUTION?

It began with a sweet wrapper, sailing through the sky,
But when I saw the look of envy in my mates, why
I knew I was on to something.
Soon fag packets were taking flying lessons
To the sighs of impressed girlfriends
And lager cans explored the principle of airborne navigation.
Things got a bit out of control:
Dealing chip papers, on windy street corners,
Inhaling car bonfires with a bad crowd,
Snorting while TVs fell from tenth-floor windows.
Eventually, we graduated to the heavy stuff –
I mean, all those politicians were up for it...
Injecting rivers,
Mainlining whole cities,
Overdosing on ozone holes.
Side effects? Countryside, animals, trees,
And a bit of a problem with oily seas.
It was a (poison) gas, the works, a total trip,
But in the end, a really rubbish relationship.

RED RIBBON – WORLD AIDS DAY

My ribbon is a
Twisted thread,
Woven for
The many dead:
Brother, sister
Lover, child,
Lives by this
Disease defiled.
With this ribbon
How we grieve,
But let us show
That we believe
This vein of life
Now running red
Links us in
A common thread.

PHARMA·SUIT·ICAL

Retrovirals? Rest assured,
If you are rich, you might be cured.
Research? Well, now, it costs a bomb,
Can't help every Hari, Dipna and Tom.
You say that we are not so nice,
But the poor must pay the price.
Protecting patents, that's the law –
Can't help the death of a few million more,
It's just business, don't you see?
Our shareholders would kill us! Honestly,
Where would the world be if we gave it away?
Here's some aspirin. Have a nice day.

FAMILY

THE PERFECT PICTURE OF TACTFULNESS

My girlfriend came round for a cup of tea,
Little sis butted in annoyingly,
"I tell you, I tell you, I tell you it's true –
Peter's got pictures of ladies like you
With no clothes on! They're under his bed!"
Silence falls. I wish I was dead.

FOR GRANDMA

Death has taken you, soft in your sleep,
Out of your hurting body, that much is true.
We are now the ones in pain, wondering why, as we weep,
Death has taken you.

Death, the breathless suitor, whispering "I do".
Mother of my mother said yes, grandfather's grief ran deep,
Husband no more to a bed-ridden bird that flew,

Flew to the far land, one of the countless many who
Were: father, brother, son – the quiet company you keep
There, where the dead in such sad interest accrue,
Death has taken you.

PETAL

My step-dad, soft as marigold petals,
Called me **his little girl**.
He built me a crab-apple tree house.
I left notes for the fairies,
Tested my bravery by jumping down.
He grew marrows, tomatoes, sweetpeas;
All was well in the garden...

I am fifteen and blooming.
Night falls,
Dark as black tulips.
His goodnight kiss,
planted on my mouth,
Has deeper roots.
He turns away,
Blindly turned on,
And my shock is a red poppy
In a field of grain
And all my love is battered by rain.

Dark Side

My
sister
curled up in
bed, skinny as a
sliver of moon.
When we were kids,
I was Dad's sunshine,
you – moonbean. But
some weird tide has
changed that happyfat
baby and in your room,
you snip at that photo
with scissors. Food has too
much gravity for you now.
At five stones, you say
you're in control, but your
eyes orbit strangely and your
body almost clanks. All the
magazines with their silver-
boned models, say it's 'lack
of self-esteem'. But our
home has always been
stuffed with love. You are
waning, almost gone from
the sky. When we were
young, I thought the
moon was made of
cheese… Our family
rises and falls with
your thin breath,
Oh my sister, my
crescent moon,
will you ever
be full
again
?

LARGIN' IT WIV ME PARENTS

He's a one-man-in-a-back-yard-division-five-team
She's a nutter-on-the-nut-roast-noshaholic's-dream
He's a taxi-on-wheels-delivery-wiv-style
She's a take-away-of-fears-servin'-up-a-smile
He's a slip-me-a-lager-just-when-she's-not-lookin'
She's a slip-me-a-fiver-'cos-I'm-really-sick-o'-cookin'
He's a walk-five-steps-in-front-don't-embarrass-me
She's a can't-go-out-like-that!-nah-yer-kiddin'-me?
He's an if-I-gotta-have-it-secret-hug-dealer
She's a dumb-down-day-bad-feeling-healer
Stir-it-together-wiv-a-nice-cuppa-tea
Laughter-on-a-plate-in-a-family-recipe.

OUR STEVE

This place I remember
Smells unlike anywhere I know.
My feet have shrunk inside these shoes.
My shirt flaps
And my hands are the size of pillows
Stuffed awkwardly into pockets.

I am not a man here.
Even the chair is instantly familiar.
As I take a seat
Resisting the urge to tip it backwards,
"Mr Richards?" I say,
Hearing my voice escape like the pop of bubblegum.
A small frown pinches between his eyes
As he glances down his list.
"Sorry, you are...?" he asks.
"Here to talk about our Steve, 7R."
I can feel sweat in the hollows behind my knees
As this man I know draws breath,
Still narrowing his eyes to fit my face.
He hasn't remembered yet.
Then he's off, telling me about
"Steve's prowess on the field"
And how he'd like him to try for the team.
He mentions casually how he'll need new boots
And the price of the kit.
I tell him I'll sort it,
And wonder silently about overtime.

He stops talking and looks at his watch

"Well... Mr...?"

"Just one more thing," I jump in,

"As his form teacher, could you...

Can you tell me how much homework he should be doing?"

He answers absently, "About an hour a night",

Looking past me to see who's next.

"OK." I nod quickly. "Thanks." And scrape the chair
    legs back.

It must be the sound that does it.

His eyes swivel sharply from my face to his list and back.

"Dan Carter!" his voice accuses,

And his finger tears holes in the silence.

"You're Steve Carter's brother!"

Like a stunned rabbit, I twitch

And try to mumble through a mouthful of old marbles.

"Good God, lad! I... you..."

He leans forward, eyes like searchlights.

"You were an absolute pain in the arse!"

And he shakes his head and then, unbelievably, smiles.

"So, Steve's your brother...

Let's hope he doesn't go the same way, eh?"

I'm standing now

Feeling my shoulders inflate beneath my shirt.

"He won't," I say,

"I'm making sure of it. That's why I'm here."

And I wipe my hand down jeans

And slowly hold it out.

KNIFE SONG

The way this ends is not with a song,
For I dream of bringing my children along
The father sang as he sat alone
Hidden in his head
In the land of the dead
And the blade of the knife lay cold as bone.

I am the feather that fell from the goose,
Down and down now I have no use
The father sighed as he sat by himself
Hidden in his head
Dreaming of the dead
And the silent knife on the kitchen shelf.

In my belly is the setting sun,
Down, down to the darkness run
The father sighed as he sat with his wife
And how she wept
As his conscience slept
And night was falling on family life.

Take the children, tucked in bed,
Father's coming to do what he said
Hidden in his heart
Is a rusty dart,
But the beds are filled with pillows instead.

Oh, the father prayed to take them all,
But the house was hollow when he came to call
They are far away,
Where it's safe to play
The feather is plucked and ready to fall.

Driven, driven to the glade,
To keep the promise that he made
Hidden in his head,
His soul now led
Down to the grove where he shall be laid.

The father whispered to the sky,
Grow me wings and I shall die,
Gripped the cable
As he was able
And like lightning learnt to fly.

Father slumped on the forest floor,
Leaf that's fallen, and what for?
Hidden in death
His last breath
Shut for ever the hoping door.

Children safe, the mother sighed,
Broken like a cup inside
Happiness cracked
And heart attacked
For daddy-o-daddy-o-daddy-o's died.

SCATTERING THE ASHES

You have gone and all that is left is words
That ring like dull bells on my tongue
And my mouth is dry
As the ashes of your body.
For one whole year
We held you in a plastic bag;
You sat, airtight, in the living room of our mother's house,
Monolithic in your black-cornered container.

Easy to say the spirit had gone,
Jumping out from your body as the last breath exhaled.
Yet in those clustered granules
Were hands I held,
Rough scraping chin,
Your gangly angularities,
The dark eyes I begin to forget.

And so we took you, my brother,
Up on to the hill,
With scissors and bags and hands,
Ready to dip into you –
The bitterest sherbert.

We found an avenue of trees,
A lane of childish days
Where women with dogs avoided us,

The weeping mother,
The cold-eyed son
Unable to comprehend the vastness of his grief.
We scooped you up
To place you at the beginning of each trunk,
An offering, a grey sacrifice,
And my mother, laden with the years,
The endless avenue of deaths,
Fell to the grass and cried out
At this ancient and Greek tragedy,

We stumbled home to finish the job
Of spreading my brother out
In the places we best remembered:
One for the wasp nest,
One for the pear tree,
One for the feast,
One for the fire,
One for the den,
One for the cut-down willow,
Where we played the perfect game of hide-and-seek.

You are hidden now,
Cut down in the maleness of your days.
My mother is made grey
By your ashes
And your terrible gift to me
Is an oldness in my youth
And the heaviness of these words
That ring like dull bells on my tongue.

A PERIOD COSTUME DRAMA

Boyfriend round for cup of tea,
Brother enters "look at me!"
With bullet belt and cowboy hat –
But, oh my God, what the hell is *that?*
"I found these bullets by your bed,
But each one has a stringy thread…
Is that where the fuse is lit?"
Enquires the brainless little git.

Oh! This life is much too cruel,
As boyfriend falls right off his stool.
There must be ways I can get rid
Of Little Bruv, The Tampon Kid.

JUST

It was **just** a dare.

It was **just** wanting to be part of the gang.

It was **just** a packet of sweets.

It was **just** not quite quick enough.

It was "**just** where d'you think you're going with that?"

It was **just** a call to the police.

It was **just** terrifying.

It was **just** after midnight when Mum and Dad came

"**Just** a youngster!" they pleaded

It was **just** a caution, at last.

It was **just**ice, I guess.

It was "**just** wait 'til you get home!"

It was going to be just like always – unfair, un**just**.

     But

It was "**just** come here, stupid!"

And after the shouting and tears, **just** a warm hug

"**Just** don't do it again, see?"

It was **just** family.

SCHOOL

DREAMING

I am a fat, curled-up comma,
Waiting in the library
And outside
The gang,
With fists full stopping at my face.
But here, I am the page
In a kingdom of words.
I catalogue the flutter of leaves
In this thought-forest.

In my head is an unwritten romance
Where ample girls are adored by men with huge
Intellects.

Now, I pause, for the singing of the bell
And the rush of gabble, gob and
gossip.
I swing into silence,
Through the long sentence of
streets
To curl up at last,
In the unhappy ending of
Home.

BALLAD OF MATT THE KNIFE

Why, oh, why did I carry a knife?
Because I was so scared for my life.
How I strutted the cruel school yard,
Bigger than the bully boys hard.

They beat me 'til I was blue and black,
My bloody nose and tooth for the crack.
But I'm a firework, watch me flare,
Now, I wonder, will they dare?

DID I-DID I-DIDDLE-I-DIE,
SHARP AS HATE AND CLEVER AS A LIE.

Then there came, there came a day,
When we put childhood away,
Tattle taunts and treasure toys,
This is the moment, come on boys!

Light the match, and stand well back,
I'm fizzing, ready to attack.
Incandescent Roman candle,
My revenge too hot to handle.

DID I-DID I-DIDDLE-I-DIE,
SHARP AS HATE AND CLEVER AS A LIE.

The fuse is lit and from each pocket,
Flies a silver-bladed rocket,
Now you'll find out how I feel,
We circle like a Catherine wheel.

Bang like a banger! Dance, he's down,
I wear the victor's sparkling crown.
But, what's this? I stagger in pain,
As from my chest flows golden rain.

DID I-DID I-DIDDLE-I-DIE,
SHARP AS HATE AND CLEVER AS A LIE.

Nothing sorted, nothing solved,
The fun and fury has dissolved,
Watch me fall without a shout,
On the ground, I am burnt out.

This bloody ballad of the knife
That did not save but snatch my life,
See my mother, father cry,
For their son, the bonfire guy.

DID I-DID I-DIDDLE-I-DIE,
SHARP AS HATE AND CLEVER AS A LIE.

IT'S ALL IN A NAME

(True story from a teacher who thought she heard a rude word)

There once was a pupil called Kerr
To whose parents it did not occur,
That naming him Wayne
Was somewhat insane,
And his classmates concurred, with:
Wayne Kerr!

MOOS AT TEN

Listen lads and understand,
This lighting of farts is well out of hand.
A scientific experiment, Shane?
To prove that cows produce methane?
How now, the poor brown cow
Light the match and BIFF! BANG! POW!
It's enough to make you wince
The sight of instant frying mince,
In fact, miss, I must agree,
It was an *udder* tragedy.

CAT'S CRADLE

I hate you and you hate me,
And though you're prettier than I,
It's not so simple. Don't you see?

We were best friends in Primary
But when I ask the stupid question why
I now hate you and you hate me,

You reply: "Silly cow! That's history!"
It makes me want to cry:
"It's not so simple". But you don't see,

No, you'd rather snog the boy I fancy
And give me the finger. I could die.
I hate you and you hate me.

Our screaming fights, though quite fist-free,
Scrape nails down cheeks as insults fly:
"You simple bitch!" And we don't see

The sudden arrival of the deputy.
Detention is nothing. I'll get by.
I hate you and you hate me.
It's that simple. Don't you see?

MR ROGERS

Let's set the scene – it was Hallowe'en.
Hanging out in the rec, feeling blue
And bored out of our skulls, nothing to do,
Remembered Mr Rogers, for a dare,
Egged each other on to give him a scare.
Bought a bunch of eggs from the corner store,
With Hallowe'en masks, we knocked on the door.
One of the gang screamed "Trick or Treat!"
Then we scrambled down the street,
But not before we managed to get
A Mr Rogers Omelette!
He went ape, it was great for the crack,
The night we launched our egg attack.

It was just for fun, we're not that cruel,
But we haven't seen him since in school.
Just a tasteless little yolk,
Can't Mr Rogers take a joke?
Next time, no treat, we'll try the trick
Of smashing his windows with a brick.

MR ROGERS 2

Too busy marking, I hadn't seen,
That once again it was Hallowe'en.
Up all night, feeling blue,
Working in the living room, as you do.
You start to wonder, What's the point?
I had reached my boiling point,
Twenty years, I've given this school,
I care about my kids, I must be a fool.
That night, quite late, the buzzer went,
Opened the door to my lads hell-bent
On treating me to their idea of a joke.
"Let's get the fat bloke!"
They chanted as they chucked their eggs,
Then ran away as fast as their legs
Could carry them. Now, I'm a mess,
Suffering from stress-related illness.
I couldn't face my class next day.
I ask you, what would I say?
Thanks to a single violent spell,
I've learned to hide inside my shell.

THE NIGHTHAWKS (AFTER EDWARD HOPPER)

This little harbour
Where bored pupils moor their boots
In the faggy mist.
School is forgotten now,
Stubbed out
As we dawdle and drag.
Trawling for laughter,
Our words are puffed out
Or held in the heart
Expelled in perfect gossiping rings.

Through the window,
In the streets,
Afternoon spills into evening
A rush-hour tide of flowing feet and faces.
The moon is a silver spoon.
Lights come on in the café.

Every word has been said now.
The chink of cup and spoon is done
As we fumble for change
And disperse like sugar
Dissolving into the caffeine city
With peppermints handy for questioning parents;
But for the moment we are sails,
Filled up with ourselves
Heading homeward
Through the dregs
Of dusk.

NOTES
FOR THE
READER

Some of the poems in this collection are based on personal experience and others (including some of those written in the first person) were inspired by listening to young people tell their own stories.

FORMS

There are many different forms of poetry used. Some of the more complex forms are explained below. Others can be looked up in a dictionary.

- Free verse – *Skate Date* (page 12), *Size Matters* (page 28), *Size Matters 2* (page 30).

- Couplets – *Within Spitting Distance* (page 7), *The Perfect Lad* (page 11), *No Way* (page 17).

- Puns – *All The Fun Of The Festerval* (page 27) is squeezed full of tabloid-style groanworthy wordplay.

- Acrostic – *I'm Not (A)cros(tic) With You At All* (page 16).

- Performance and rhythm – *Performance Pressure* (page 34).

- Ballad – *Matt the Knife* (page 84). This poem, like many ballads, has been set to music. It was inspired by tragic events in the news, and recollections of teenage fights.

- Villanelle – *Cat's cradle* (page 87). This form of repeated lines echoes the unending and bitter feuds that can destroy school years. Tercets with a quatrain (four-line stanza) finish. The rhyme scheme is ABA ABA ABA ABA ABAA. The first and third lines of the first stanza are repeated at the end of each stanza in different order until the last quatrain, where these two lines make up the final couplet.

- Shape poems – *Up To Speed* (page 52), *Dark Side* (page 72).

- Sonnet – *Under My Skin – Self Harm* (page 22). Andrew met this girl briefly while working in a school. Without thinking, she had rolled up her sleeve, revealing the dreadful gouges in her arm.

- Roundel – *For Grandma* (Andrew's grandmother) (page 70). Made up of three tercets on two rhymes with a repeated refrain, this form reflects the circularity of life and death.

- Extended metaphor – *Petal* (page 71) uses the imagery of flowers.

- Pantoum – *Sorry Am I Repeating Myself?* (page 54) This poem is made up of quatrains with lines two and four in stanza one repeated as lines one and three in stanza two and so on. The final stanza puts lines one and three of stanza one as lines two and four. The pattern of repeating lines mirrors the state of mind.

PERSONAL NOTES

French Verbs (page 19) is based on Polly's French exchange experience.

Quiz Yourself (page 36) is loosely based on an actual teen magazine quiz.

The Naming Game (page 38) – This poem is based on the sexism of expletives.

Many of the poems in the *DRINK AND DRUGS* section are based on Andrew's teenage years. *First Drink* (page 44), set at an outdoor inn in the hills of Slovakia, at a family reunion, is written in half-rhyme, the form capturing the swaying blur of the subject matter.

Mad For It (page 56) takes as its premise the word 'mad' with all its different connotations and uses. It is an accurate description of Andrew's own experience.

Minimum Wage (page 60) – Back in 1987, Andrew worked as an exhausted and very broke barman in Bristol for £2 an hour.

1948 (page 61) is about Andrew's mother, Vera Fusek. She was a Czech refugee in 1948, unable to return to a country that would kill her father and imprison her family. It took ten years for her to gain naturalisation (a British passport) and she was regularly insulted on the street. As the UK is made up of so many different historical and cultural backgrounds from Roman, Viking, Norman to more recent immigration, the authors felt ashamed of how this country treats incomers. They wanted to ask the question – What defines being British?

Andrew's stepfather, Rudi Krejci was part of the student movement when the communist coup happened in Czechoslovakia in 1948. In order to avoid arrest, he hid in his parent's house for five years, in a small space above the pantry. His escape as described in the poem may seem unreal but is totally true. Having spent five years reading philosophy books in the pantry, he later became a real *Professor Of Philosophy* (page 62).

Papers (page 64) – In 1985, Prague (in former Czechoslovakia), was still under communist rule, with a heavily armed police presence.

Condom (page 40), *Red Ribbon* (page 66), *Scattering the Ashes* (page 78), *Pharma-suit-ical* (page 67). Andrew's brother Marc, died of AIDS in 1993. See also *Plays With Attitude – Angelcake* and *Poems With Attitude* (Hodder Wayland).

Our Steve (page 74) is based on a true story told to Polly.

Knife Song (page 76) – Autobiographical. See also *Plays With Attitude – Dragon Chaser.*

A Period Costume Drama (page 80) – It really happened!

Dreaming (page 83) – If the dreaming girl reads this, she'll know who she is.

Moos At Ten (page 86) – The exploding cow urban myth is still alive and well!

Mr Rogers (pages 88-89) is not his real name. This teacher told his story on the radio.

The Nighthawks (page 90) – This recalls a café on a street corner where afternoons drifted by after school. Edward Hopper painted luminous pictures of places. 'The Nighthawks' is one of his most famous pieces, which perfectly captures the atmosphere of the café.

ABOUT THE AUTHORS

Andrew Fusek Peters works as a performer and writer-in-education, visiting schools around the UK. He also works extensively in television.

Polly Peters is a former English and Drama teacher who also works as a community theatre director.

Between them, Polly and Andrew have written and edited over thirty books, many of them critically acclaimed. You can find out more about them by visiting: www.tallpoet.com